The Pueblo

The Pueblo

Charlotte and David Yue

Houghton Mifflin Company Boston

Library of Congress Cataloging-in-Publicaton Data

Yue, Charlotte.
   The Pueblo.
      Bibliography: p.
      Includes index.
   Summary: Describes the history, daily activities, construction of dwellings, and special relationship to the land of the Pueblo Indians.
   ISBN 0-395-38350-1
   1. Pueblo Indians—Juvenile literature. 2. Indians of North America—Southwest, New—Juvenile literature. [1. Pueblo Indians. 2. Indians of North America—Southwest, New]   I. Yue, David.   II. title.
E99.P9Y83   1986   85-27087
979'.00497

HC ISBN 0-395-38350-1
PA ISBN 0-395-54961-2

20   19   18   17   16   15

To our parents

Contents

The Pueblo

The People and the Land

CHAPTER ONE

The People Who Lived in Pueblos

The Southwest is spectacular country. Nature has carved the land forms into magnificent sculptures. Steep, multicolored mesas give way to deep canyons, and vast areas of dry land with a sparse growth of stubby grasses reach out toward the high, snowcapped mountains in the distance. It is beautiful country, but it seems a harsh and forbidding place for people to live. Wide stretches of desert are separated by rocky cliffs. The climate offers droughts, sandstorms, flash floods, and blizzards. But the Pueblo Indians and their ancestors have lived there for so long that it is as if they have always been there.

About thirty pueblos are still inhabited today by Pueblo Indians. The Hopi village of Old Oraibi has been inhabited continuously for longer than any city in the United States. Pueblo people have been building villages, cultivating crops, and making beautiful pottery since the time of Christ. And their hunter-gatherer ancestors were living in the Southwest thousands of years before that.

Long before Columbus arrived, civilizations flourished and elegant stone masonry cities were constructed high in the walls of sheer cliffs. The people had developed techniques to farm the dry land of the region. They grew crops for their food and cotton to weave into clothing. The pottery and baskets they made for serving and storing their food were works of art. They were very religious people; their cycle of ceremonies was devoutly performed every year. Governments with many officials saw to the smooth running of the community. Irrigation systems built by some communities had canals twenty miles long. The system supplied water to several villages, the flow controlled and directed by mats made of woven fiber.

Their houses — built from the stone, clay, and mud at their feet — were frequently almost indistinguishable from the hills and mountains that surrounded them. They appeared to be outgrowths of rock formations on the mesas where they were built. These villages were made up of clusters of box-shaped, flat-roofed dwellings often piled five or more stories high. There were no doors on the ground floor. Ladders that could be

pulled up if there was trouble led to hatchway entrances on the roof and to upper levels.

The name *pueblo* comes from the Spanish word for town or village. The people who lived in these villages are called Pueblo Indians, although many distinct Indian groups are included in this term. Pueblo people spoke different languages and had different customs, but they all lived in villages, built similar dwellings, made their living by agriculture, and had similar beliefs and a similar way of life.

Pueblos are often compared to apartment houses, but that description is misleading. We design and construct even the largest apartment building as a whole. We set the outer limits of a building and divide that into smaller spaces with floors and walls. To the Pueblos, a room was a complete house, and a building was really a collection of separate houses, each built and owned individually. A house could be added next to or on top of another house as more space was needed, or a house could be taken away without the whole structure being significantly altered. The overall structure was constantly changing.

These clusters of houses were built around open spaces usually referred to as "plazas," although a Pueblo plaza was not at all like a European plaza. It was not a place for markets or fairs, for social gatherings or public announcements. It was a large, open-air room for the religious activities of the community, the place where the public dances and ceremonies took place. In all as-

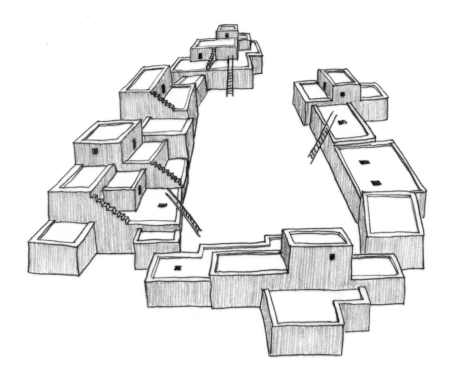

pects of life, Pueblos harmonized their practical needs with their spiritual needs. By building their houses around the plaza, people could sit on their terraces and watch the dances, but they also built their houses around this spiritual room as an expression of devotion.

At one time Pueblo groups were living throughout the vast area of the Southwest. During their long history, tribes moved frequently in search of safer and more fertile sites for their villages and farms. The Spanish explorer Coronado first encountered these unique villages when his expedition journeyed through the southwestern part of North America in 1540. By that time the Pueblo settlements were mostly scattered along the Rio Grande and its tributaries. The Hopi and the Zuñi were the only Indians who continued to live in desert country near the homes of their ancestors. Those in the Rio Grande had arrived there long after the Hopi and the Zuñi were well established.

There have always been marked distinctions between desert and river pueblos. The Hopi land is the most forbidding and arid of any pueblo, and the Hopi villages on the mesas were the most isolated. *Mesa* is the Spanish word for table, which describes these flat-topped land formations well. The villages stand on three steep, rocky mesas that jut up into the desert. For a few weeks in early summer, wildflowers brighten the landscape; but for most of the year, there are large areas that cannot support a blade of grass. There is no river near them, and the Hopi had to depend on un-

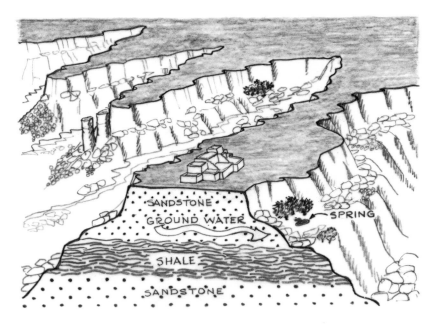

derground springs and summer thunderstorms to supply the water for all the villages. Because their land is the harshest and most remote, they had the least contact with outsiders.

Zuñi, to the east of Hopi, has a more varied landscape. It has a stream, but an adequate water supply was still a constant concern. The Zuñi pueblos were built in open valley sites at the foothills of the mesas. The Zuñi people's way of life, like the Hopi's, remained close to that of their ancestors.

Acoma and Laguna are usually included with the desert pueblos. They were situated in barren country and were isolated from other villages.

The rest were river pueblos. River pueblos differed

from one another in many respects, but having a constant water supply and a somewhat more fertile environment made them stand in sharp contrast to the desert pueblos. Most river villages were not near rocky country, and the houses were built of earth.

In desert and river pueblos alike, villages gave protection from enemies, and communities answered the spiritual and social needs of the people. Homes were built from the meager materials at hand and were well adapted to the difficulties of the environment.

The Environment of the Southwest

The Pueblos lived in the southwestern portion of what is now the United States. Ruins of their cities and villages are found in parts of five states: Arizona, New Mexico, Utah, Colorado, and Nevada. By the time of the arrival of Europeans in this area, their settlements were mostly in New Mexico along the Rio Grande. A few stretched out across the state toward Zuñi near the western border. Farther west, in Arizona, were the Hopi villages.

This country is varied, but it is all semi-arid or arid land, and drought was always a constant danger. Some of the land is hot, dry desert. Much is mountain tablelands. Most of it is rocky or has a sandy, clayey soil. Some of the valleys are well watered but not always well suited for agriculture, being too narrow and having too short a growing season. Many of the streams and rivers dry up for months at a time.

There are strong winds, especially in the spring, little humidity, and many cloudless days of intense, glaring sunlight. Rainfalls can be heavy, but the rain is quickly absorbed into the dry, clayey earth and evaporates quickly in the dry atmosphere. The heavy rains are followed by months of almost no moisture. The temperatures range from scorching midday heat to very cold nights.

But the landscape is truly beautiful, and the Pueblos found a way to live in harmony with nature. Mountains were holy places, houses of gods and supernatural spirits. Lakes and springs were sacred and were often seen as doorways to worlds below this one. Worship entered

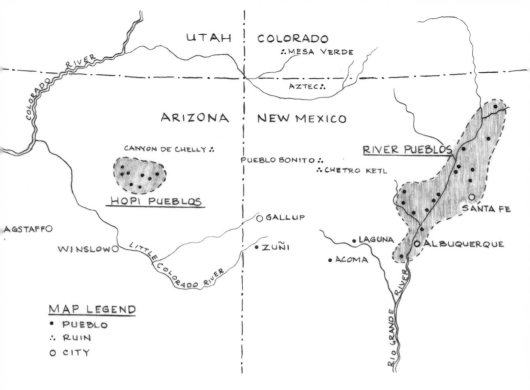

into every part of the relation between the Pueblo people and their land.

A History Told by the Land

Pueblo Indians believe that the first home of their ancestors was a world below the earth. They moved up to higher planes until they reached the surface of the earth at Sipapu, the sacred place of emergence. The earth is the fourth plane on which mankind has existed. People and families were arranged by clans, given what they needed to survive on earth, and assigned pathways.

9

Then the people journeyed south and established their villages.

Different Pueblo groups may tell the story in a somewhat different form or have a slightly different word in their language for the holy place where they emerged. But all share a basic belief that the earth gives everything life; we are all part of the earth and must all share the earth to live.

Preserved in the earth are clues that can tell us many things about the history of these people and their journeys through the land. The earth of the Southwest is a good preservative; things tend to dry out rather than decay in such an arid climate. The ruins of the buildings they once occupied tell a story, and the mounds where they discarded rubbish show in what order things were made and used. The things on the top of the pile are usually from a more recent time. Pottery is especially useful because the pottery of each area and time period is distinctive.

We can determine dates fairly accurately with a tree-ring calendar. As a tree grows a ring of new wood is added every year, the new wood always at the outside of the trunk. In wet years the ring is thick, in dry years it is thin. The general series is the same for all trees of one kind in the same location. If we cut down a tree and count back from the year it was cut down, we can give a date to each ring. By comparing this with a sample slice of a tree cut at an earlier time, we can carry the dates farther back. The tree-ring calendar of the Southwest

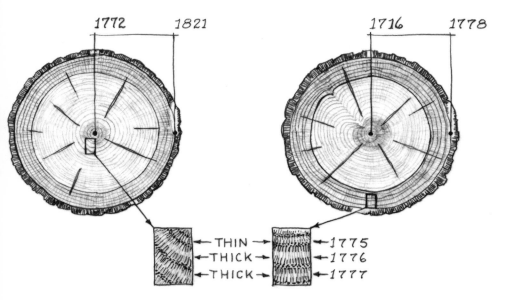

1772   1821   1716   1778

← THIN →   ←1775
←THICK→   ←1776
←THICK→   ←1777

now stretches back to the first century A.D. We can determine the age of buildings by dating beams with this calendar. We can also learn about the amount of rainfall in past years. Timbers found in ruins are studied with the scraps of pottery, basketry, dried corn, and charred wood found nearby to learn how long a building was occupied and what things were used during that time. From these objects archaeologists piece together the history of the Pueblo people.

We know that by at least 5000 B.C. there were people roaming the Southwest, hunting and gathering wild seeds and plants. They found shelter in caves or put up temporary arrangements using boughs of trees to protect themselves from the elements. They made baskets to carry the gathered food and milling stones to grind roots, seeds, and berries into flour and paste.

Sometime between 1500 and 1000 B.C. they learned to grow small ears of corn. It took over a thousand years, but gradually corn made important changes in their way of life. As their farming techniques improved, they could depend on a regular crop. They did not need to wander so far to have an adequate food supply. They now had to spend more time in one place, tending their gardens and fields and guarding the food they were able to reserve. Other inhabitants of the Southwest were hunters who roamed the region in search of food. This in turn led to the need for more permanent dwellings and safe storage places.

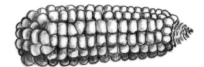

ANCIENT CORN

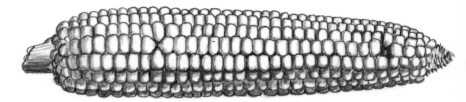

MODERN CORN

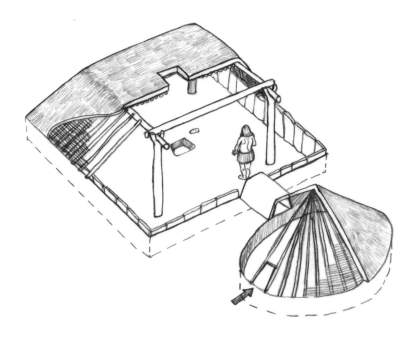

At first they probably lived in caves in the sides of cliffs and dug pits to store their corn. Later they dug larger pits that they could live in. They excavated a shallow pit and built walls of upright poles, filling in the spaces with mud or completely covering the wall with mud plaster. The roof was made of timbers, brush, and twigs and plastered with earth. By being sunken in the ground, these houses were protected from heat and cold.

Several families began building houses together. Over the centuries, as their farming became more successful, they had more time for working at other pursuits. They learned to make pottery, and their ability to make good storage and cooking utensils encouraged

further agricultural development. In time, they improved their corn and started growing squash, beans, and cotton. They began decorating the pots they made; pottery became artistic as well as utilitarian. They learned to use bows and arrows and to weave cotton into cloth. They developed methods for building houses using the stones that were plentiful in that region.

The direct ancestors of the Pueblo people are usually called by the Navaho name *Anasazi,* which means "the Ancient People." The harshness of the land forced them to move many times during their long occupation of the Southwest. They built homes, planted crops, and remained in one place for many seasons until drought, disappearance of a spring, soil exhaustion, disease, fire, flood, or warfare forced them to move and rebuild their homes in a more promising location. Tribes would separate; other groups would meet and band together. Most villages were made up of many separate groups, and the members of each group had their own traditions and had arrived by their own path while following omens from the gods and pursuing a place to live and farm in this inhospitable environment. They occupied successive stone villages. These were well designed for defense from enemies and people who might try to steal their food supply, and stone was the best material for the environment and the most readily available.

From about A.D. 1100 to 1300, about the same time the great cathedrals were being built in Europe, the

MESA VERDE

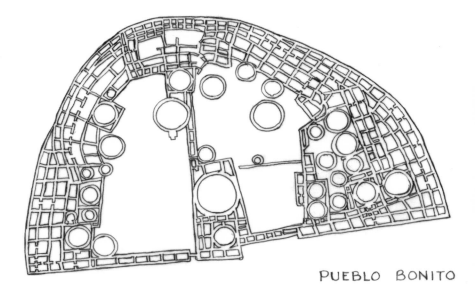

PUEBLO BONITO

Anasazi constructed their most magnificent buildings. During this period many beautiful stone cities were built in the part of the country known as the Four Corners — the area where the states of Utah, Colorado, Arizona, and New Mexico meet. Pueblo Bonito, Chetro Ketl, and Aztec Pueblo were built in river valleys. Careful planning enabled the Anasazi to make their villages safe and defensible. These villages were compact, the many stories of the great buildings rising like steps forming a high outside wall with almost no openings. Some, like Mesa Verde and Canyon de Chelly, were built in cavernous recesses high in the walls of cliffs, out of the reach of enemies.

Fields of many-colored corn, squash, and beans surrounded the villages. Reservoirs and ditches stored flood waters for drier times. Men wove beautiful cotton garments, and women made elegant pottery. They worked in stone, made jewelry, and traded with many people and tribes throughout the wide area. Their religion was already a central part of their lives, and all the villages had underground rooms for ceremonial purposes.

After about two hundred years the great houses were deserted one after another. Probably many things happened to cause this, the most important being a drastic change in the amount of rainfall. For twenty-two years, from 1276 to 1298, there was almost no rain. Four Corners had once had several streams and just enough rain to ensure a crop if the water was used carefully. The streams dried up, and the area became desert. The people moved again, drifting toward the fertile valley of the Rio Grande.

When Coronado and his expedition first came into Pueblo country, they reported the existence of between sixty and seventy villages along the Rio Grande. Juan de Oñate came in 1598 with colonists to settle in the Pueblo country and to teach Christianity to the Native Americans. Priests imposed a system of forced labor and tried to supplant the faith of the Indians. Sacred dances and rites were prohibited and religious societies and orders abolished.

In 1680 all the Pueblo Indians rose in revolt and drove out the Spanish. Even the Hopi and the Zuñi, who suffered less because they were more secluded and inaccessible, joined them. It was the only time the Pueblo people formed a union. The Spanish did not return for twelve years. These, however, were twelve hard years for the Pueblos. In fear of retaliation from the Spanish, many moved and reconstructed their villages in more secure sites high on the mesas. There was fighting with the Navaho and the Apache. Crops failed.

When a new Spanish governor, Diego de Vargas, was appointed in 1692, widespread rebellion ceased. More and more white people moved in, some taking Indian land. As always happens when different people are mixed together, there was learning and sharing of ideas. The Pueblos began cultivating new crops — wheat, chilies, peppers, cabbages, and onions. They began growing melons, apricots, peaches, and other fruits. Some raised sheep and were soon weaving wool instead of cotton. They learned to knit and embroidery techniques improved. Bone needles were replaced with steel ones. The Pueblos added new colors to their work that had not been possible with the vegetable dyes available to them. They learned to mold adobe into bricks and how to build fireplaces and chimneys.

Mexico gained independence from Spain in 1823, and in 1848 the pueblos came under the jurisdiction of the United States. Railroads came through in the 1880's, bringing many people into the area and with them new materials and ready-made goods. Many Pueblos began making less of their own pottery and doing less of their own weaving as dishes, utensils, and cloth became easily available. The United States government forced Pueblo children to attend schools that had been set up to teach American ways. Anthropologists, archaeologists, and other scientists began studying life among the Pueblo communities, giving us some of the best information we have about Pueblo life. Buildings changed with the introduction of furniture, modern tools and equipment, and glass for windows. Houses began to look less and less like the ancient villages. Some villages changed drastically, others more slowly.

The Pueblo way of life has persisted even though it has changed and developed. Throughout their long history, Pueblos have learned from Indian people to the south, from Mexicans, from the Spanish, from the Navaho, from Plains Indians, and from white Americans. Each new idea or resource was adjusted to the needs of Pueblo life and combined with materials and ideas already in use.

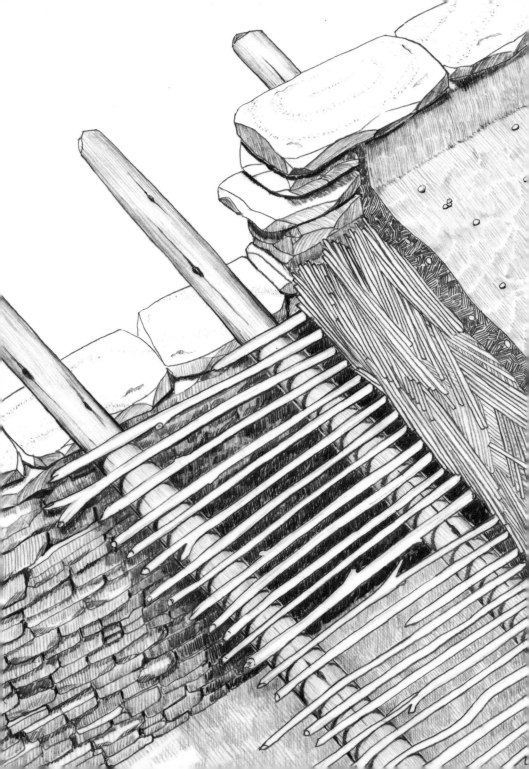

The Structure of Pueblo Dwellings

CHAPTER TWO

Materials and Tools

Building materials came from as nearby as possible, since the chief means the Pueblos had of transporting materials was to carry them on their backs. In the desert pueblos of the west there was an unlimited quantity of sandstone. Mesas are formed of this soft yellow or red rock, which could be found at the bases of cliffs throughout the tablelands. Sandstone looks as though it is formed of grains of sand cemented together, and it breaks very easily. With only their stone tools, the men could work the slabs into smooth, thin blocks. Nearly all the ancient pueblos were built of sandstone masonry.

In the eastern river valleys stones of any kind were scarce, so houses were often made entirely of earth. There is a special kind of earth called adobe in Arizona and New Mexico. Adobe is a sandy clay. When wet, it can be molded and shaped easily. It does not crack or shrink much in the drying process and becomes a very hard, uniform mass. Ashes were sometimes added to improve its performance as a building material. Adobe was used in all pueblos for mortar and plaster.

The timber for roof beams was the only material brought from a distance. Wood was not easy to get. When it could be obtained, it was difficult to work and shape with the available tools. Men had to go to the mountains to find timbers and used whatever kinds of wood they could find.

Tools for chopping and hammering were made from very hard stones that did not split easily. The toolmaker would choose a piece of stone close to the size and shape he needed for his tool. Then he chipped it roughly into the shape he wanted by striking it with another piece of stone. He then shaped and polished it until it had a smooth finish. To obtain a sharp edge, he would wet the stone tool and carefully and patiently rub it on a flat stone sprinkled with sand until the edge of the tool was smooth and had the shape he wanted. Grooves were formed in an ax or hammer so that a wooden handle could be tied on with a leather thong or strips of yucca fiber. Pueblo men used this kind of tool to cut down trees for building the roofs of their houses.

Tools for smaller cutting jobs were made out of stones that were brittle and split easily. To shape and sharpen these tools, he pressed a piece of bone against the edge of the knife and tapped it with another stone until a flake chipped off. He would keep chipping off flakes, making a scalloped edge. Such a knife was usually triangular in shape, about three inches long, and had a handle tied on. It resembled a long arrowhead.

Deer bones could be formed into picks and chisels with very little shaping. The pick used for breaking out the stones for house building was usually a heavy stone about a foot long which had been pointed and sharpened. Wood was smoothed and shaped with pieces of sandstone.

Pueblo men kept a selection of tool materials and sandstone slabs of different sizes in their storerooms. During the winter or when they had the time, they would sit outside and work on their tools.

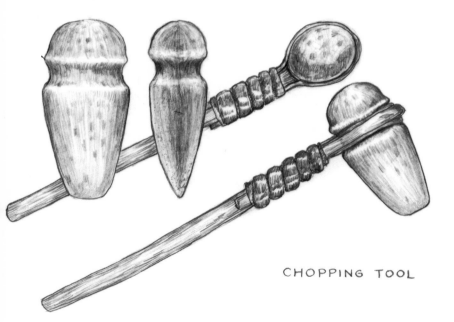

CHOPPING TOOL

Division of Labor and Ownership

In pueblo construction, men were usually the masons, and women were usually the plasterers. But sometimes most or all of the building was done by a woman and her female relatives, and sometimes men and women worked together on all aspects of the construction of a house. Making the roof was generally done by women, although men often helped to lift the heavy beams into place.

In most pueblos the completed house belonged to the woman. Children belonged to the clan of their mother. The oldest daughter's house was regarded as home by her brothers as well as by her nieces and nephews. A man went to live with his wife's family when he married. In a few pueblos, houses could be owned by men.

The upper terrace in house clusters was a common area, not owned by anyone. It was a place for social gatherings, conversation, and taking the air.

Ceremonial rooms, or kivas, were constructed by religious organizations responsible for particular rituals. Men belonging to that religious society did most of the labor. Women did not take part in kiva activities and were rarely allowed to enter the kiva, but they helped with its construction and upkeep. When the roof and floors were completed, the female relatives of society members went over the interior walls, bringing them to a smooth surface and filling in openings with small stones. Then they plastered and sometimes white-washed the walls and the inside of the hatchway. Women would come into the kiva once a year to go over the plastering of the interior walls.

As a rule, each Pueblo man or woman made the equipment and tools he or she would be using. Women made their grinding stones, their fireplaces, and their ovens. Women made pottery and baskets; men did the weaving, knitting, and embroidery. Men made the hammers, knives, and arrows they needed in their work. Men also kept a lookout for promising stones to bring home which might make good tools and equipment.

Men were the field workers, and crops that were standing in the fields belonged to men. Once the harvested food was brought to the village, it belonged to the mistress of the house; she would dry, sort, and store it. It was her responsibility to discard food that had become moldy and dry it again when necessary. She used the corn and other dried goods for food, sold it, or gave it as gifts as she thought best. A man needed permission from his wife to dispose of food himself.

Seeds were the property of the family. These were carefully guarded and given away only when a man married. When he went to live with his wife's people, he brought some of the cherished seeds for the first planting of his wife's fields.

Range and grazing land belonged to the community. Trees and streams and wild plants, no matter where they were found, belonged to everyone.

Masonry Construction

A single rectangular, box-shaped room was a complete house. There was no overall plan for the arrangement of houses or multiple stories. Houses could be added as more space was needed. Pueblo people lived together in clans. When a man married, he moved in with his wife's family; when the married couple needed their own home, a site close to her family's dwelling was chosen. It might be next to her mother's house or perhaps next to an older married sister's.

The first step in building was to gather the materials. The man would go to the mountains and cut timbers for the roof. Piles of stones were gathered and cut roughly to size. Friends and relatives would help with all parts of the construction and were given their meals as payment. This was such a large expense that people tried to build with as few helpers as possible.

As with most things in Pueblo life, housebuilding was accompanied by prayers and ceremonies. The Pueblo religion was very much a part of everyday life. When a house was to be built, the man went to the village chief and asked him to prepare prayer feathers to protect the house and those who would live in it. The chief would take four small eagle feathers and tie a short cotton string to each. He sprinkled sacred meal on them, offering prayers for the house and the welfare of its occupants.

CORN FIELDS

PUEBLO

CORRALS

RAINWATER POOL

KIVA

SPRING

FIELDS

GARDENS

CORN FIELD

PEACH ORCHARD

FIELD SHELTER

CORN FIELD

CORN FIELD

SPLASH STONE

ELEVATION

STONE FLOOR

HEARTH

FLOOR PLAN

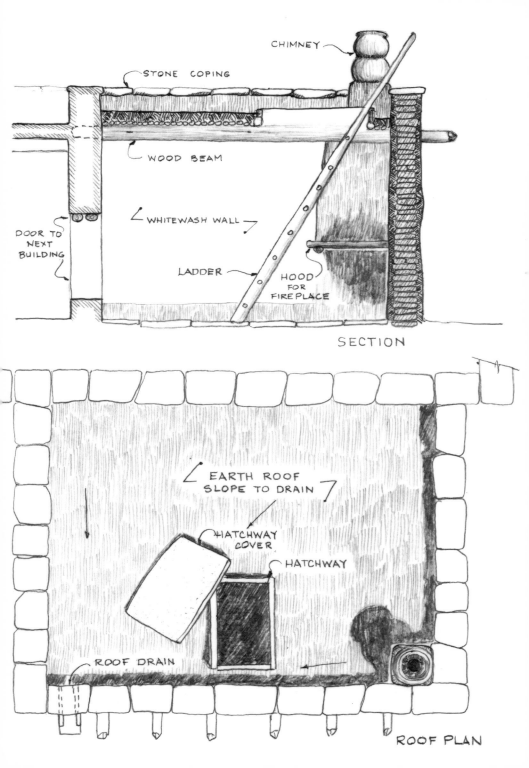

CHIMNEY

STONE COPING

WOOD BEAM

WHITEWASH WALL

DOOR TO
NEXT
BUILDING

LADDER

HOOD
FOR
FIREPLACE

SECTION

EARTH ROOF
SLOPE TO DRAIN

HATCHWAY
COVER

HATCHWAY

ROOF DRAIN

ROOF PLAN

The man would place one of the prayer feathers at
each of the four corners of the house and cover each
with a large stone. Then, to mark the lines where the
walls would be, he sprinkled a mixture of corn meal,
crumbs made from a special paper-thin bread, and
herbs. As he did this, he chanted an ancient housebuilding song. This ceremony was observed for any ground-
floor addition to the house, but it was not necessary to
repeat the ceremony if additional stories were added.

The site was generally not prepared in any other way,
and the stones of the masonry were set directly on the
surface without excavation or foundation of any kind.
The surface was solid rock and difficult to prepare with
the tools available to Pueblo builders. Walls were laid in

courses, continuous layers of stone, using as little mud mortar as possible. An opening was usually left so the workers could move in and out during construction, but this was closed up before the walls were finished. The completed walls were about seven or eight feet high and between twelve and twenty inches thick. Often the wall varied in thickness from one part to another because of the irregularity of the stones.

After the large stones forming the main body of the wall were laid in place, the spaces between them were carefully filled with smaller stones and fragments sometimes no more than a quarter of an inch thick. They were embedded in the mud mortar and driven in with stone hammers. This brought a smooth surface to the wall. Some walls had remarkably smooth, even surfaces, but this depended on the neatness and care with which the chinking was done. Older masonry often had close and careful chinking with countless small tablets of stone.

Pueblo builders had few logs available for beams and no tools capable of cutting logs into boards, but they managed to work out a system for building a strong roof. The method rarely varied. The roof was constructed of at least four layers, each crossing the layer below.

The first layer was the principal rafters. These were straight, round logs of pine or cottonwood about six to eight inches thick. The bark was peeled off and any

projecting knots were removed, but the housebuilders did not try to square up the logs since they had only stone tools to do the work. These beams were laid across the walls about two feet apart. The ends were left sticking out. The length of the main beams determined the width of the house. Since it was difficult to get long tree trunks and drag them to the village, houses were rarely more than fourteen feet wide. An average house was about twelve feet by twenty feet.

The main beams were crossed by a series of poles going the long way. These poles were pine, piñon, cottonwood, juniper, or willow, about one and a half to two inches thick. The bark was stripped from the poles and they were laid close together, a foot or less apart, leav-

ing an opening if a hatchway entrance was needed. The ends of these smaller poles were embedded in the masonry of the walls.

The third layer crossed the second. In this layer were small willow branches or reeds, placed as close together as possible. Then the women crossed another layer above this of grass, weeds, small twigs, and brush. They spread a layer of mud over this framework and allowed it to dry completely. Finally a thick covering of dry earth was put on top and the women tramped it down until it was smooth and even and firmly packed. The roof was like the ground itself, and it served as a front yard to dwellings that opened on it. Skins might be pegged out to be tanned and dried there, and outdoor ovens were sometimes built there.

The walls were then carried up to the height of the roof surface and often a few inches higher. The walls were capped by a protective coping. This consisted of thin, flat stones laid close together to cover the top of the wall as completely as possible. This protected the wall from violent rains. Very thin stones were used that could be easily trimmed to make the coping as smooth and uniform as possible.

In many villages the woman would coat the outside of the house with mud plaster the consistency of modeling clay. This adobe covering was smoothed over all the rough places a handful at a time.

During the rainy season, storms did not last long, but

they were often extremely violent. Heavy rains or standing water could easily wear away the masonry and the earthen roof. This erosion was prevented by roof drains, spouts that helped to get the water off the roof as quickly as possible. Usually a long, narrow stone slab was inserted in the coping. It projected from the wall, slanting down to direct the flow of water off the roof and away from the walls. Improved drains had sides added. These directed the water more effectively. Small hollowed-out tree trunks, a curved half of a gourd, an old pot, or discarded grinding stones might also be used. If the spout from an upper terrace drained onto the roof below, the lower roof and walls were protected by thin slabs of stone known as splash stones.

When the roof was finished, the woman spread a thick coating of mud for the floor. Sometimes the man would pave the floor with stone blocks, filling in the cracks with adobe. This kind of floor was easier to sweep and keep clean, but it added weight in upper stories. In Pueblo buildings, the floors are the ceilings of the dwellings below them. Bits of earth often crumbled and fell to the room below, especially if the floor above was paved with stone.

Another ceremony was performed when the walls, roof, and floor were finished and the outside walls had been plastered. Crumbs were sprinkled along the rafters of the house. This was called "feeding the house," and the Pueblos believed it brought health to the people living there. Four more prayer feathers were made by the village chief at this time and they were tied to the central roof beam with prayers for the safety of those under the roof.

Adobe Construction

In the river pueblos, where stone could not be obtained, adobe became the main construction material. The Pueblos have been using adobe in their construction for almost as long as they have been building. One of the old ways of using adobe was to burn a large pile of sedge grass and sagebrush twigs. When this had almost finished burning, they threw water on the fire and added earth to the ash mixture to form a stiff clay. This was made into round balls that became very hard as they dried. These hardened mud balls were used instead of stone and fixed in place with more of the same mixture.

Another method was to mix the adobe in a large batch and build up the wall in sections. Two frames were made of poles woven with reeds or grasses. Each frame was about five feet long and about three or four feet high. The two frames were stood as far apart as the desired thickness of the wall and filled in with adobe. When the filled section had dried, the frames were moved and another section of the wall was built. The process was repeated until the walls were completed. If enough small stones were available, Pueblo builders might not use supporting poles. They would make a stiff mixture of stones and adobe and build up the walls in layers. They would let each layer dry in the hot sun, patting a new course by handfuls onto the dried part below until the walls reached the desired height.

Adobe walls were built only as thick as necessary, rarely more than a foot thick. Some Pueblo builders did not add any ash. They just waited for the rainy season and used the adobe as it was taken from the earth. But this material was not as durable, and during the rainy months these buildings needed constant repairs.

The Spanish introduced the idea of adding straw to adobe and of using wooden forms for molding the adobe into bricks. The mold for the bricks was a rectangular box without a top or bottom, divided into sections the size of individual bricks. Usually each brick was about 10″ × 14″ × 4″ and weighed about thirty to thirty-five pounds. The mold framework was placed on level ground. Adobe was mixed with water and straw and packed firmly into the mold. When the bricks had set, the form was removed and they were left to bake in the sun for a few days. From time to time they were turned and stood on the narrow ends so that they would dry completely. When enough bricks had been made, the foundation was prepared.

The foundation for an adobe house was a shallow trench filled in with stone. The foundation had to go below the frost line, below the level to which frost would penetrate the earth. The walls were built up, using more adobe mud for mortar. The roof and the rest of the building were made by the same methods as in stone masonry construction. When the house was completed and dried, it was covered with a smooth coating of adobe plaster.

Maintenance and Upkeep

Adobe is very hard when it is dry, but it will eventually crack and wear away. Heavy rains are particularly damaging. The Pueblos had to take care of any places that were eroding. The outside plaster of adobe houses was renewed every year or two. Masonry dwellings that had plaster on the exterior walls also required the same frequent upkeep.

A woman did her plastering during the rainy season. She would scrape loose plaster off the wall, moisten the wall, and smooth on a new coat of plaster with her hands, covering all the rough places. At this time she would also give the floor a thin wash of adobe mud if it did not have stone paving. Some people mixed fresh animal blood with the mud because this made a much harder surface.

Every other year she would also whitewash the inside of her house. Some people think Pueblos learned about whitewash from the Spanish; others say it was in use before the Spanish came. Whitewash is made from gypsum, another of the riches of the Southwest. The man would dig out the white crystals from one of the deposits he knew of and pound them into fragments with a stone. His wife would cover the fragments with cattle dung, bake them, grind them again, and store them ready for use. After the rainy season, when there was plenty of water, she mixed water with her gypsum.

Some women just used the lumps of gypsum as they came from the earth and dissolved them in hot water.

A woman smoothed the whitewash over the walls using a piece of sheepskin or goatskin as a brush. She did not whitewash completely down to the floor. She left a band of brown adobe plaster about ten inches wide, somewhat like a baseboard, because the white around the floor would get soiled by the floor dirt. In a few villages this whitewash of gypsum was also used on outside walls.

Another important part of taking care of a Pueblo home was the renewal of the prayer feathers tied to the central roof beam. Every year four more feathers were prepared by the chief, and the ceremonies and prayers for safety were repeated. This was as important to a Pueblo as an insurance policy is to a homeowner today.

How the Structure Was Designed to Perform Well

Pueblo builders knew only one way to build. Pueblo structures changed over the years, but at any given time, people were building the way they had seen others do it before them. The architecture that evolved during the long history of the Pueblos performed well in this difficult and harsh environment. Pueblo homes successfully withstood heat, cold, wind, sandstorms, and violent rainfalls and comfortably sheltered people from hot days, cold nights, and intense, glaring sunlight. The Pueblos accomplished this by making the best use of what they had.

The materials available were earth, stone, reeds, and saplings. Stone and clay absorb solar heat during the day and slowly release it during the night. This kept the temperature inside the building even and comfortable both day and night. The massive roof was particularly good for absorbing heat. The door and window openings were all very small, thus reducing the glaring sunlight and solar heat during the daylight hours. The whitewashed walls reflected heat and light and helped brighten the room in spite of the few windows.

The outside temperature averaged about 105° in the afternoon and 65° at night, while the temperature of the roof surface averaged 140° in the afternoon and 70° at night. Inside, however, the temperature was maintained at a comfortable and fairly constant level. The

inside temperature ranged from an average of 80° to 85° in the late afternoon and early evening to about 75° in the early morning.

The homes of the Pueblos also offered protection from enemies. Often this was achieved by building on a site difficult to reach, but in many cases they had to rely on their architecture for protection. Houses were built close together around a central plaza with only narrow covered passageways to enable people to move through the crowded clusters. Having small windows and few

door openings aided in the defense of a pueblo. The lack of any openings on the ground floor and the removable ladders probably saved villages on many occasions.

In the course of the Pueblos' long history in the region, the difficult character of the land forced them to keep moving in search of more favorable locations. But over the years of building and rebuilding, their architecture advanced and they learned to build homes that performed well and were well adapted to the land.

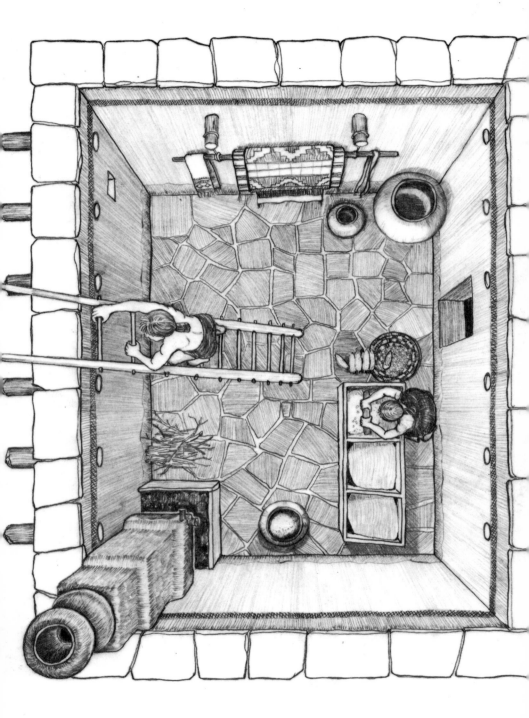

Life in a Pueblo

CHAPTER THREE

Interiors, Furnishings, and Details

"Up the ladder and down the ladder" was a Zuñi phrase meaning "to enter a house." If we went up the ladder and down the ladder, we would have found a small, dark room, brightened only by the sunlight that came through the hatchway and the glow given off by the fire. This one room was the home of the entire family, but Pueblo families had learned to make their houses neat and well organized.

Most of the furniture in the Pueblo dwelling was built in. Masonry ledges were built along opposite sides of the room about three feet from the floor. They looked like long, low benches, but they were shelves for storage. Sometimes a small storage bin for grain or beans was built by setting one or two stone slabs into the floor, cutting off a corner of the room. Often the shelves and bin were covered with mud plaster and white-washed like the surrounding walls. The fireplace was built in another corner. The blackened cooking pot used for stewing food would be kept beside the fireplace along with some gourd dippers and dried, hollowed-out gourds that were used for bottles and containers. A broom made from gamma grass tied together usually stood near the fireplace. The long, soft ends were for sweeping the floor, and the short end of the broom was used as a hairbrush. When the broom became short from wear, it was used to brush the metates or the hearth.

An indispensable part of every Pueblo home was the

trough containing the metates. These were the milling
stones used to grind the corn. The trough was built in
or near one corner and arranged so that the women
could kneel behind it, facing the middle of the room as
they worked. The trough usually had a series of three
grinding stones, which were separated into compart-
ments by thin slabs of sandstone. Each grinding stone
was about three inches thick and fixed into its compartment in a slanting position. The stones were arranged
from the roughest to the smoothest, and the corn was
ground on each one in turn, becoming finer each time.
The first stone was basalt or coarse lava, the second a
coarse sandstone, and the last a fine sandstone. On each
of the metates was a cylindrical stone the width of the

slab, called a manos, which the women or girls rubbed up and down over the grinding stones.

A woman needed to grind three or four quarts of flour almost every day. She took dried kernels of corn off the ear and crushed them as well as she could on the coarsest stone of the metates. As the corn grew sticky, she toasted it over the fire. The process was repeated on each of the grinding stones until the corn had been reduced to a fine flour. Sometimes women and girls would work together, one at each stone.

She also had a mortar for grinding and pounding other foods, such as seeds and dried fruits. The mortar was a stone hollowed out in the middle, and a stone with a rounded end was used as the pounder.

With such a small living area for each family, the room had to be kept uncluttered. Storage spaces were important. Along one side of the room a straight pole might be suspended from the roof beams, or its two ends embedded in the walls. This was the clothes rack for hanging garments, blankets, and robes when they were not being used. Deer horns might be attached to the wall to hang clothing or other household items. Sometimes there were niches in the walls, left when the house was built or made by walling up a door or a window. These became cupboards for storing the bowls for mixing and serving food and for small odds and ends. Large jars full of water were kept in a corner of the room. Parts of the equipment for weaving might be built into the floor as pieces of the regular furnishings.

There were no tables or chairs. Dishes were placed on the floor. The family sat on the floor to eat or used folded or rolled blankets as seats. There were no beds either. Blankets, rugs, or sheepskins were spread on the floor at night for sleeping and hung on the clothes pole in the morning.

Hatchways

It was not until the 1880's that doors began to be seen on the ground floor. Before that time rooms were entered through hatchways, large trap doors in the roof. Hatchways were originally designed as a defensive feature. It was a good way to protect the food that was stored in the ground-floor storerooms from raids by other tribes and to protect the people from enemy attacks. Ladders led from the ground to the roof and from the roof down into the rooms. The ladders could be pulled up if there was trouble, leaving the enemy facing a blank wall.

Upper stories often had doors, but upper-story rooms also sometimes had roof openings to provide light or to give access to rooms without connecting doorways.

The hatchway was incorporated into the roof construction. The distance between the two main beams where the hatchway was to be built determined the width of the opening. The second series of poles was interrupted at the sides of the hatchway and the builder arranged all the other layers of the roof so as to leave the space for the hatchway open. She finished the sides with carefully laid small stones and mud plastering. Then she placed a narrow stone slab on each of the four sides of the opening to protect the plastering from rain damage, as she had for her roof coping.

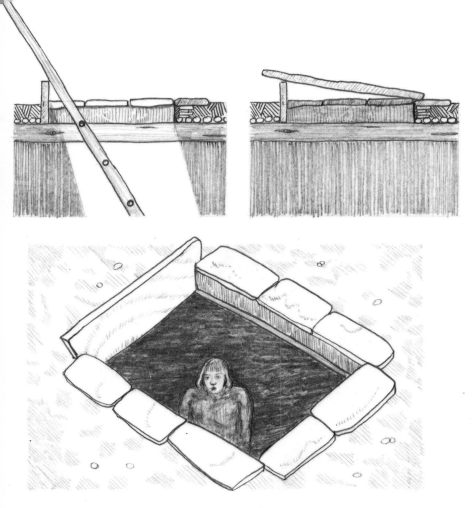

A thin slab of sandstone was used for a cover when it
rained or when there was a sandstorm. Sometimes one
of the stone slabs around the opening was set on edge.
When the cover was placed over the opening with a
high slab at one end, the sloped cover shed water away
from the opening, but some light and air could still get
into the room below.

Doors and Windows

For protection against enemies and the elements, Pueblo Indians tried to keep the openings in their dwellings — doorways and windows — as small and as few as possible. Also the available door closings at that time were either cumbersome or did not seal the opening well from the wind and the cold. Sometimes doorways were closed by a large slab of stone set on edge. Others were closed by blankets or rabbitskin robes hung over them in cold weather. A curtain pole was frequently built into the door jamb two to six inches from the top to hang the door cover.

In Pueblo buildings there was not always a clear distinction between doorways and windows. Most doorways were really only large windows. Doors were usually three and a half to four feet high. The bottom of the doorway was raised about ten inches above the floor. People had to step over the door sill when entering. This was also true of inside doorways connecting rooms. People naturally bend when they must step over something, so this step really made the small size less uncomfortable.

Not all doorways were rectangles. Many had a wide opening at the top half of the door and a narrower opening at the bottom. Sometimes the door was a T shape, and sometimes one side was stepped and the other straight. Even when both sides were stepped, one

step might be higher than the other. Pueblo people carried loads of food and fuel in on their backs. These irregularly shaped doorways served to keep openings as small as possible while still allowing a person carrying a bundle to move through easily. And the curtain pole above the door was also a convenient handhold when going through a door.

Movable wooden doors were probably introduced by the Spanish. They were usually made of a single panel enclosed by a wooden framework. The panel was fitted into grooves in the frame which had been carefully cut out with a small knife. A hinge was worked into the door itself. One sidepiece of the frame was longer and shaped into rounded pivots at the top and bottom.

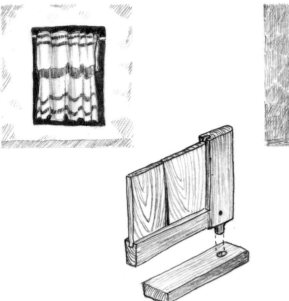

These fitted into round sockets carved in the top and bottom of the doorway.

Some openings served as windows, intended only for light, air, and looking out. The openings in a room were placed where they were needed, so they were often of different sizes and at different heights from the floor.

To frame a window, a space was left in the wall. Small cedar poles were then placed side by side across the opening in the masonry where the top of the window would be. This was usually the only support for the stones and earth above. Sometimes the weight of the wall would bend the poles. This was another reason to keep openings small. There were no jambs or sills of any kind, only the masonry on the sides and bottom of the opening. Using boards as frames came later from Spanish or United States influence.

During the 1880's glass began to be used, often set directly into the adobe without any window frame. Before glass, windows were sometimes filled in with selenite. This is a clear variety of gypsum which splits easily into layers. Slabs about an inch thick were carefully fitted together and held in place with sticks set in the adobe.

In some of the crowded house clusters, inner rooms had no openings to the outside. To get light into these rooms, an oval opening was made where the roof joined a wall. This opening was carried down at an angle between the roof beams, enabling a little light to come into the room. But this also let some rain into the room.

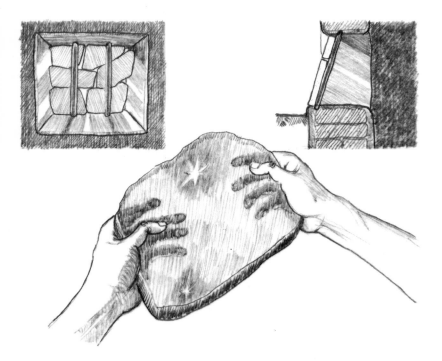

Doorways and windows were often adapted to meet changing needs. Doorways were changed into windows; windows were made larger or smaller. New openings might be broken through walls, and new rooms sometimes shut off windows, which then became cupboards.

OVAL WINDOW

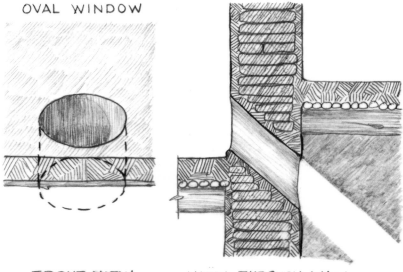

FRONT VIEW   VIEW THROUGH WALL

Doorways and windows were often sealed up to save fuel and keep warmth in during the winter or if the family was away for a long time. Often families moved to farming pueblos for a month or so at the planting and harvesting seasons. They would fill in the doors and windows either with rough masonry or with a thin slab of sandstone plastered in place.

Ladders

The earliest ladders were just logs with notches cut in them. These were still being used as late as the 1880's, although other improved ladders were also in use. For the simplest ladders, notches were dug in the vertical pieces and the rungs were fitted in and secured with rawhide or yucca fiber.

Later, holes were made through the sidepieces and long rungs were slipped through both sides. In times of danger the ladder could be left in place and only the rungs had to be pulled out. That was convenient, but such ladders were not very stable. To prevent the sidepieces from spreading apart, they were inserted into a crosspiece at the top of the ladder. This was a piece of wood with a hole near each end. The sidepieces of the ladder were made extra long and were tapered at the ends. These narrow ends fitted into the holes of the crosspiece. Crosspieces were often decorated with carvings or notched designs. Ladders usually had eight rungs; some had as many as twelve.

In very crowded areas, double ladders were sometimes used to help with the traffic. Double ladders had three vertical pieces instead of two, and rungs were made long enough to go through all three. All the sidepieces fitted into one crosspiece made with three holes.

In Hopi, ladders were rarely used above the first ter-

race. Since stone was easier to obtain than wood in those pueblos, stone steps frequently led from the first terrace to the upper stories.

Women with jars of water on their heads, men carrying loads on their backs, and children bringing firewood with playful dogs at their heels had to make their way up and down these ladders. Considering how difficult this must have been, it is not surprising that some ceremonies intended to protect children from accidents were performed at the foot of ladders and that women gave feather offerings for safety and luck in ladder climbing.

Fireplaces and Chimneys

Ancient buildings had only a pit, used both for cooking meals and for heating the house. It was located in the center of the room so that everyone could easily gather around it for warmth and so that smoke could escape through the hatchway. By the nineteenth century houses had a fireplace and chimney, and the hatchway no longer served as a smoke vent. When a house was built, the fireplace and chimney were added after the house was considered complete, after the ceremony to feed the house had been performed and the prayer feathers were in place. We can tell from this that the fireplace and chimney were relatively recent developments. It was difficult for Pueblos to fit new ideas into the traditional way of doing things, and they often kept them outside the ancient ceremonies. The chimney and fireplace may have been the result of Spanish influence, but they developed and improved over many years.

The first change was surrounding the cooking pit with a wall high enough to protect the fire from drafts. Later the fireplace was moved to a corner of the room and a hood and flue were added. This was an improvement in getting smoke out of the house. With the fireplace in a corner, the two walls could give the structure support; and the smoke hole was no longer the same opening that was used for an entrance, exit, and source of air. The fireplace and chimney were built by women, in keeping with the Pueblo idea that people build what they would be using.

The woman planned for the chimney as she was building the house. She placed a heavy pole across the corner of the room into the masonry about three feet from the ground. This would support the flue. She dug a pit in the earth floor in the corner under the pole and made a hole in the roof directly above the fireplace.

In building the flue she used the materials and techniques she knew. She used basketry materials for the framework and then covered this with mud plaster. The technique was also similar to methods used by some ancient builders for roof construction. She stood sticks or large sunflower stalks on the supporting corner pole

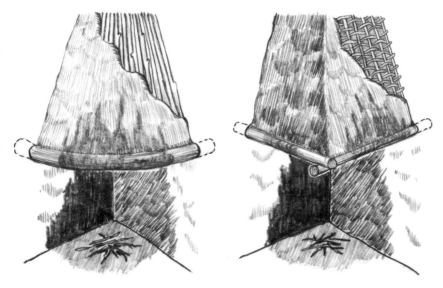

ONE POLE HOOD   TWO POLE HOOD

and arranged them at a slant coming together at the smoke hole. Some women wove this as they did their wicker baskets. When the framework was in place, the woman plastered the inside and outside with a thick coat of clay. The finished flue looked like a canopy, and it served to lead the smoke out the smoke hole. A later improvement was a corner hood supported by two shorter poles instead of a single pole. This formed a rectangular hood and allowed room for a larger fireplace.

Such a structure would have been dangerous with a very hot fire, since the clay might break off and the framework would burn easily. But fuel was scarce, and Pueblos were careful and economical in using it. Fires were fed with tiny sticks, and cooking depended on simmering the food slowly rather than searing it on a high flame.

Making a fireplace in an upper-story room was a problem. The fireplace needed to be a foot or more deep, and the floor of one room was the roof of the room below. They managed to get a pit of sufficient depth by building up the sides with stones.

The family did not depend on the fireplace to heat their room, even though it did add some warmth. For the most part they relied on sealing off drafts, on moving to ground-floor rooms, which were easier to heat, and on the warmth of many people gathered close together.

The external chimney was very likely a result of

Spanish contact. Originally the chimney was just a hole
in the roof, but it was gradually improved. First the
sides were raised above the roof, forming a round or
rectangular shaft. Eventually the chimneys were given
height by adding a chimney pot or as many as were
needed to make the fire draw properly. Pueblo women
knew how to make use of anything they had available.
The pots were ordinary household utensils that had
been damaged in some way. They were black cooking
pots with burned-out bottoms, large-mouthed jars,
or broken water jars or other vessels. The upper pot
overlapped the one below it, and they were held together by a coating of adobe cement.

67

Water

The harsh environment taught Pueblo people that it was essential not to waste anything. They learned to take advantage of every possible means of increasing their water supply. Villages along the Rio Grande had a perennial water source that supplied some water for irrigation, but drought was a constant danger for the desert pueblos. All pueblos needed rain as well as streams and rivers to keep their fields moist.

Prayers, dances, and ceremonial games were an important part of ensuring a water supply, and these rit-

uals were practiced in great earnest. The people also constructed reservoirs to collect and store rainwater and drainage waters from the mountains. Natural basins in the rocks were dug out as much as possible and then walled with masonry. Some of these reservoirs were as large as 110 feet across and four feet deep. Desert people used to get the village together whenever there was snow on the ground, and everyone would roll huge snowballs and put them in these basins. They could get a large quantity of water from the gradually melting snow.

Storage

Careful preserving and storing of food was essential for the Pueblos' survival. They tried to have a year or two of food stored in case of drought. When there was not enough rain, the whole crop for the year could be lost. The climate was naturally good for drying and preserving, and they built stone chambers that could be secured fairly well from the ravages of hungry rodents. Dark inner rooms of house clusters were ordinarily used only for storage. Here the corn was stacked in piles neatly sorted by color and by quality. All the winter foods — the dried fruits, vegetables, and meats — were stored here, as well as the clay, basketry materials, firewood, and stones to be worked into tools and household equipment.

In the autumn, after the harvest, every available space in the pueblo was used to dry food to preserve it for later use. Terraces and copings were covered with ears of corn, fruit, and strips of squash, pumpkin, and meat. Every projecting beam or stick had drying foods hung from it. Long poles were positioned between any available spots as temporary drying racks. Even many ladders had extra crosspieces added to serve as places to hang strings of drying vegetables. Ears of corn were braided together by their husks and hung to dry.

Extra storage areas were sometimes needed. Two forked poles were stood upright in the ground near a wall. Using crosspoles and branches, a rough platform was set up between the forked poles and the stone coping of the wall. Ears of corn were tossed there to dry. At other times of the year, such a framework might be used for storing firewood. There were few trees near the pueblos, and it was important to keep a good supply of fuel.

After special ceremonies a sprig of evergreen or a prayer feather was placed in the storage room for extra luck as the food was stacked away.

Family Life

Pueblo families lived in one room, but most of their daily activities were out of doors. Their homes were used mainly for sleeping and for being sheltered from bad weather. The terrace was an outdoor kitchen and sitting room. The women went up and down ladders to outside ovens on the terrace or down on the ground. The outdoor drying racks had to be tended, and baskets and pottery were often worked on outside.

The workday began at the first light of dawn. Pueblo people hung up their bedding and everyone washed up. They worked first and ate later. The men would start off to the fields, and the women would sweep the floor and begin preparing the day's food.

Children learned by helping. Boys worked with their fathers and uncles. They would go together to the fields. Younger boys scared away crows or gathered up brush. When a boy was old enough, his father might let

him work a plot by himself. Girls worked with their mothers and aunts, grinding beside them at the grinding stones. Even small children would be asked to bring some sticks of firewood. Grandfathers worked on their weaving and often taught the children, giving instruction in what was right and wrong and why. Or the wisdom of their years might entitle them to a ceremonial office or a place in the town council. Grandmothers might still do some of the pottery work. They also gave advice and helped take care of the children.

The men took leftover bread with them to eat in the fields, and the women might have some leftovers for a late morning meal. The workday ended in the late afternoon. The men returned from the fields, and the family sat on the floor and shared the main meal of the day. The evenings were spent talking, laughing, and visiting neighbors. At dark the blankets were again rolled out on the floor for sleeping.

When a ceremony was approaching, there would be more activity, with extra cooking to be done, costumes and prayer sticks to be prepared, and announcements from the town crier about the coming events. On the day before the ceremony, the whole family would wash their hair with soapweed. Many friends and relatives from other pueblos visited to watch the dances, and people wore their best clothes for the occasion.

In winter the men would spend the days working on tools, weaving, and searching for fuel. Winter evenings were times for storytelling. There were special winter ceremonies that helped the sun turn back, brought the snow, or prepared for the planting season ahead.

Other Structures

CHAPTER FOUR

Kivas

All pueblos, even the most ancient, had rooms that were different from ordinary dwelling rooms. They were usually larger, often circular rooms, built underground, and placed in an important spot within the pueblo. Such a special room is known by the Hopi word *kiva,* meaning "ceremonial chamber." Much of the spiritual activity of the community took place in the kivas. The public portions of ceremonies were performed in the plazas, but the private portions were held in the kivas.

In Hopi villages these large underground rooms were recognizable by the long ladders sticking out of the openings. Circular kivas aboveground, with a ladder or stairs leading to a roof entrance, were the most common kind in the Rio Grande pueblos. At Acoma and Zuñi the kivas were special rooms within the house blocks.

Housebuilding techniques have changed and improved, but many of the ancient ways were preserved in these religious structures. People want to hold on to the traditional practices associated with what is sacred. From kiva building we can learn something about the earliest construction practices and trace the developments that have taken place in building methods.

Originally kivas were built to enclose and protect the most sacred objects and ceremonies. On the floor of the kiva was a sacred cavity called the sipapu. The sipapu was the place where the spirits or power of the gods entered the kiva. Houses were built around the kiva to enclose and protect it. In an ideal plan the terraces would all face the court so that the people could watch the masked dancers, the kachinas, as they came out of the kivas to perform the ceremonial dances in the court. Women and spectators from other pueblos gathered on the terraces and sprinkled corn meal on the dancers as they listened to the dancers' songs.

This ideal plan could not be used on all sites. On Hopi mesas it was not possible to dig into the solid rock with the available tools. To build an underground kiva, the Hopi people had to use natural cavities that needed little excavation. These were usually found near the edges of the mesa, where there was not enough room to build the houses around them. The traditional arrangement of the kiva within the enclosed court was given up in order to have the kiva underground. An-

cient kivas were usually circular, but on rocky building sites this was not considered as significant as building the kiva underground.

The Pueblos believed that a balance between spiritual and practical purposes was important. Kivas were built underground in imitation of the original home beneath the earth in which they believed life began. But subterranean kivas were also practical because they were cooler in the summer and easier to heat in the winter.

In Zuñi, during the Spanish occupation, forbidden ceremonial rooms were hidden in inner parts of the crowded house cluster. Here floors were sometimes dug out below the ground level. The Spanish and other outside forces had greater influence on the river pueblos, and they have held on less to the ancient practices in building both houses and kivas.

Kivas were built by the religious societies that held their sacred observances in them. The size of a kiva depended on the number of men who would be using it and on the kinds of rituals and ceremonies that would be performed in it. Usually they were about twenty-five feet long and half as wide. They were about five and a half to eight feet high.

After the excavation had been made, the kiva chief performed the same ceremony as the male head of the family did when building a dwelling — placing the prayer feathers, sprinkling the crumbs, and chanting. Walls of stone masonry were built along the sides of the excavation even when the kiva was constructed completely underground. Building ceremonies marked the position of the walls and placed prayer feathers beneath the cornerstones. To keep the rituals, the Pueblos felt it was necessary to build walls even when the excavation had natural stone walls. The masonry walls were carried up to within eighteen inches of the surface. The main roof beams and the second series of poles were laid in place, leaving an opening about five feet by seven feet for the hatchway. The kiva hatchway had stone walls resting on the roof beams. Hatchway walls were carried up at least eighteen inches above the ground, one side higher than the others, forming a slope. The rest of the roof was completed using the same method as for a house roof. The packed mud of the final layer of the roof was made level with the ground.

A kiva hatchway served as the entrance, exit, smoke

vent, and window of the kiva. It needed to be large enough to permit dancers wearing elaborate costumes to get in. Sometimes a crosspiece was placed across the hatchway, dividing it into unequal sections. The smaller section was directly above the fireplace and served as the smoke hole, and the larger section was the doorway and window. The masonry walls of the hatchway helped prevent fire and served the purpose of a chimney. A reed mat or a stone slab or a combination of the two was used to close the kiva hatchway when necessary.

Inside the kiva the walls were smoothly plastered. The floor was covered with stone slabs. One end of the kiva had a platform extending the full width and about one third of the length of the kiva. The platform was about ten or twelve inches higher than the remaining part of the room. This was where women or visitors sat when admitted to witness a ceremony in the kiva.

At the other end of the room, opposite the platform, there was a low masonry shelf about a foot wide to display sacred objects. A niche was built in the wall be-

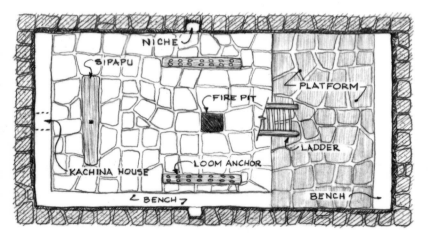

KIVA PLAN

hind this to hold masks during certain festivals. This was called the kachina house.

In the floor near the end of the room was the sipapu, the most sacred part of the kiva. This was the symbolic representation of Sipapu, the place where the people emerged to the surface of the earth. It was also the place of contact between the natural and the supernatural worlds. A cavity was made about a foot deep and ten inches wide. This was covered by a piece of cottonwood cut to fit level with the floor. There was a small hole fitted with a wooden plug in the middle of the cotton-wood plank. Sacred figures were set around this spot during the festivals.

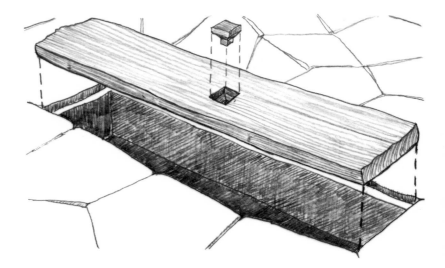

To some Pueblos the kiva also symbolized the four worlds that man occupied. The cavity beneath the floor represented the place of beginning, the main floor represented the second plane, the platform signified the third level, and the outside was the world now inhabited. The ladder always rested on the platform, never upon the main floor, symbolic of the coming from the third plane into this world. Men came out of the kiva and danced as their first ancestors had danced when they reached the surface and found the earth to be good.

Many kivas had ledges along the side walls for benches, and there were niches in the side walls for sacred pipes and other small articles. A fire pit, about a foot square, was made directly under the hatchway. Sometimes loom attachments were built into the kiva, since it also served as a workshop for blanket weavers.

River pueblo kivas had a fireplace toward the east with an altar behind it and the sipapu in front of the altar. A shaft at floor level led to the outside. This served as a ventilator shaft to keep the kiva well aired. The altar served as a deflector, protecting the fire from drafts. Its spiritual purpose was to provide entry for the spirits who mingled among them, gathered smoke, and carried the smoke through the hatchway.

When the construction of a kiva was completed, the kiva chief performed the ceremonies to feed the house, and there was a time of feasting and dancing. At this time the kiva chief proclaimed the name by which the kiva would be known.

Sacred observances were held in kivas, but the kivas

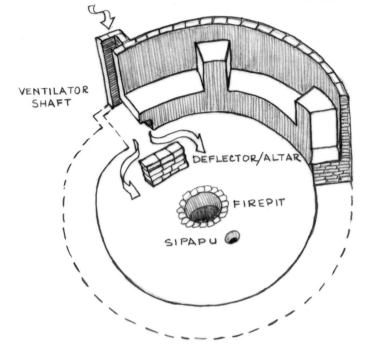

VENTILATOR
SHAFT

DEFLECTOR/ALTAR

FIREPIT

SIPAPU

were not used only for religious purposes. Council meetings to discuss public affairs were held there. Kivas were workshops for weaving and other manly arts and places for men to meet and relax. Every man had a membership in a particular kiva, although there was visiting among men of different kivas. Women were not allowed to enter kivas except to plaster the walls and for occasional ceremonies. Usually one kiva was the main kiva of the village and had the most elaborate ceremonies performed in it. The kiva chief was in charge of all kiva matters and membership. This was usually a hereditary office. On his death the oldest son of his oldest sister would become kiva chief. In most pueblos kivas were closed to visitors and many felt it impolite for strangers even to walk past these sacred places.

Stoves

Most of the cooking was done out of doors, and various structures were built for that purpose. The simplest was the cooking pit, which was a hole dug in the ground and lined with mud. Some were walled with upright slabs of stone with the edges often sticking up six or eight inches above the ground. Cooking pits were about a foot across and eighteen to twenty-four inches deep. Sometimes women made a little tunnel about three or four inches wide going diagonally from the ground to the cavity. They could tend the fire through this opening without reaching directly into the cooking pit. A fire was built in the pit, and when the pit was hot enough, the fire was allowed to burn out. After all the ashes had been swept out, the food to be cooked was put in. The top was covered with a stone and sealed with mud. The food was left undisturbed for about twelve hours, and it would be nicely cooked.

Pueblos were vegetarians most of the time. They ate meat when they could get it, usually rabbits, gophers, or squirrels. Men went on regular hunting expeditions for larger game, such as deer, antelope, mountain lion, or fox. But this was not just to get meat. These animals also provided important equipment. Pueblo people needed sinew for thread, bowstrings, and fasteners; skins for drums and some clothing; bone for tools; and hoofs for ceremonial rattles.

At harvest time corn, beans, squash, and other foods were cooked fresh. But for most of the year the people ate dried vegetables and fruits. This diet was supplemented by gathering the fresh plants that were available at different times of the year — wild roots, berries, piñon nuts, yucca fruit, and the fruit of the prickly pear. Almost all Pueblo foods used some corn meal. Pueblos had about forty ways to cook corn.

The Spanish showed the Pueblos how to make a dome-shaped oven. It was usually called a beehive oven because of its shape, or by the Spanish name *horno*. The woman would lay out a circle of stones for the foundation. Then she built the oven in courses, laying the stones in mud mortar, leaving a door about eighteen

inches square at one side. Since the walls of the structure curved inward, she let the mud dry before adding
the overhanging portion. She finished it with a smooth
coating of plaster on both the inside and the outside.
When completed, it stood about four feet high. Like the
cooking pit, it could not hold both the fire and the food
to be cooked at the same time. The fire was built, the
oven heated. Then it was swept clean. The food was put
in, the opening sealed, and the food left to cook slowly.
This oven was generally used to cook small, round
loaves of bread.

Sometimes small rooms called piki rooms were built
just for making the special paper-thin bread called piki.
Piki rooms were about seven feet wide, ten feet long,

and five to seven feet high. There was a chimney and hood in the corner of the room over the special stone stove. The stove consisted of a long, flat sandstone tablet held up by two slabs of stone that were embedded in the floor. The fire was built under the sandstone tablet, which was used somewhat like a griddle.

It took a day to prepare the sandstone as a piki stove. It was heated very gradually; any sudden temperature changes would cause the tablet to crack. The surface was rubbed with oil, usually from sunflower or squash seeds, but buffalo fat was used if available. This was alternated with treatments of gum from the piñon tree until the tablet had a polished black finish. The process was accompanied by a ceremony to prevent the stone from cracking. It was believed that if a single word was spoken during certain parts, the stone would crack. When the ceremony was finished, the stone was scrubbed with twigs of pine or juniper.

To use the piki stove, it had to be heated again very gradually and an even temperature maintained. The fire was carefully fed with small bits of fuel. The batter was poured on the stone to make paper-thin bread. Piki was made once every week or two and stored in a special box. Piki crumbs were used in housebuilding ceremonies. Piki was eaten at ordinary meals, provided for travelers or field workers, and given to performers at dances and ceremonies.

Corrals

The Pueblos raised sheep, cattle, and horses. In more recent times some villages began raising oxen, pigs, burros, goats, or chickens. Where possible, the corrals for the animals encircled the pueblos. On rocky sites the corrals were placed wherever suitable space was found on the outskirts of the village. They were usually roughly rectangular enclosures constructed partly of stone masonry. The other sections of the corral were made of stakes and brush that were held in place by horizontal poles tied with rawhide. Forked poles were

sometimes braced against the horizontal poles to steady the structure.

In some villages small corrals were built near houses as cages for eagles or other birds. Birds were valued more for their feathers than as food. Eagles were the most valuable, and rabbit hunts were as important for getting meat to feed the eagles as to feed people. Before wool was introduced to the Pueblos, they twisted wild turkey feathers and yucca string into long ropes and used basketry techniques to make the ropes into warm winter wraps. A man could not have too many feathers; they were an important part of Pueblo life. Feathers could carry prayers to gods and spirits and were used in most offerings and ceremonies.

Gardens

Every family had a small plot near the village. Corn, squash, and melons — the main crops — were grown on larger fields located farther from the village. The small gardens were for special crops: peppers, beans, cotton, onions, chilies, or maybe a special variety of tobacco. The Pueblos tried to find a place near water for the little gardens — for instance, under a drip or beside a stream that might at least have water underground if not above. These gardens were carefully tended and during dry seasons were watered by hand. Since water was so scarce, the Pueblos built ridges of earth around each plant to hold in the precious water, each plant standing in a separate compartment. The neat ridges formed little, regular squares like waffles, so the small plots have become known as waffle gardens.

Pueblos constructed walls to protect the gardens from hungry animals. The walls were about two and a half to three feet high and about six to eight inches thick. The construction was done quickly, using lumps of adobe rolled into balls and plastered with mud. The walls needed frequent repairs, but they also could be broken down quickly to make it easier to get into the gardens at harvest time. After the autumn harvest, spaces were often left in the walls so that animals could feast on the remains.

Farming Villages

It was difficult to find good locations for fields in this harsh climate; that required careful observation and judgment. Knowing where the flood water from summer rains would come rushing down from the hills was necessary. But places where the flow was very strong and might bury plants would not be good. Gentle slopes below rock or shale or valley floors were good places. But even in a good location the flow of water needed to be controlled, and farmers built small dams out of earth and brush to direct and hold the water. This network of dams was always in need of repair and care. Desert farmers sometimes built dams around separate plants to control the strong torrents that came with summer flooding.

Desert farmers had perfected their methods of dry farming. Any moisture in the dry clay earth was deep underground. They had to plant their corn deep so that the roots would be able to reach the water. It was also important not to disturb the hard crust that covered the earth because that sealed in any moisture that was there. It was always difficult to determine where underground moisture was located. The Pueblos planted a special variety of corn with long roots that could get to deep moisture and short, tough leaves that could withstand high winds. It was hearty enough to resist most droughts and had a short enough growing season to

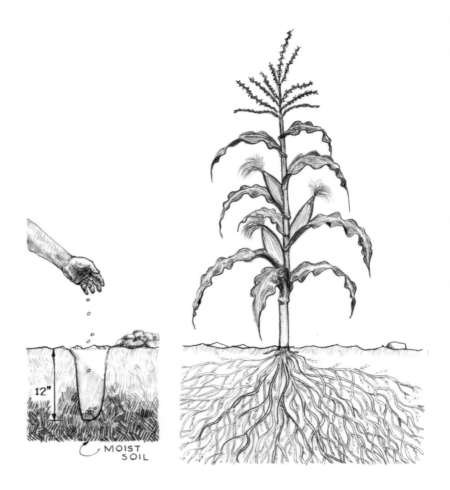

ripen between the last frost of spring and the first frost of fall. Farmers made deep holes using a digging stick and planted about twenty kernels in each hole, hoping to ensure at least some survivors.

Even with all this, everyone had to have fields scattered in many parts of this barren land. If one field failed, another might succeed. This meant that the main fields, which needed constant attention, were often at a distance from the village. Sometimes the men ran the miles to the fields. Villages had competitive racing games and ceremonies, and running to the fields was one way to train for the events.

Some families camped in the fields for the farming season. Sometimes they would occupy the remains of an ancient settlement, making enough repairs to make it livable. Or they built farming villages, quickly and roughly constructed for temporary occupation. The families would remain for the planting and harvesting and move back to the main pueblo for the ceremonies and stay until spring.

Those who went daily to the fields sometimes put up light shelters for the children working in the fields and for refuge from the blazing sun. The shelters were built of brush or stone or whatever material was available.

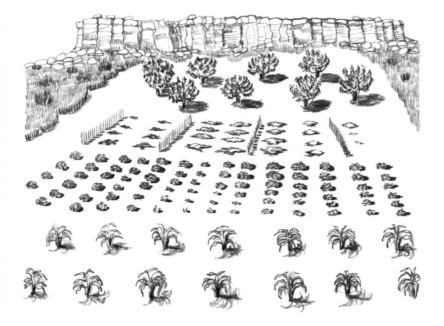

For one kind of simple field shelter, ten or twelve cottonwood saplings were set in the ground to form a curved enclosure. Leafy boughs were laid against them and held in place by horizontal branches that were attached to the cottonwood saplings.

For a more elaborate retreat, forked poles were arranged upright in the ground to support a flat roof of poles and brush. A wall of upright branches enclosed one or two sides of the shelter, extending high enough to shade the roof.

Churches

Churches were established in all pueblos by the Spanish. The Spanish usually insisted on their own building styles and construction techniques. Churches were almost always built of adobe bricks, even the ones in villages constructed of stone masonry. The bricks were made in the Spanish method, straw being mixed with the adobe. In Acoma a beautiful adobe church was built under the direction of the Spanish, but the Pueblos had to haul all the clay for the adobe up the steep cliffs from the valley below.

The Pueblos learned from the Spanish while building these churches for them, but it is questionable how much of a lasting impression the churches and Christianity had on the Pueblo people. Certainly it was kept apart from their beliefs and religion and did not replace their own ceremonies. The churches, though built by Pueblo labor and often quite magnificent, were really Spanish buildings.

Pueblo Communities

CHAPTER FIVE

Plans of Different Communities

The Pueblos were village people. It would be very difficult to find just one house standing by itself. Houses were built in rows or clusters or blocks of several houses piled in steps. The overall plan of the village was not thought out before any families began to build, and no outer limits were set. The arrangement that took shape answered the social needs of the community. Each individual house met the needs of one family unit. The house units were organized to fulfill the cultural and spiritual needs of the group as a whole.

Just as the Pueblos' lives were centered around their religious beliefs, their homes surrounded plazas. Plazas were like outdoor rooms for spiritual activities. Ceremonial dances were performed in the plazas. Often a

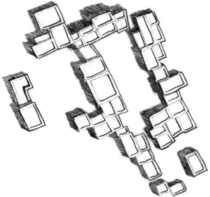

PLAZA

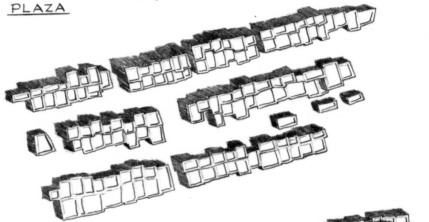

STREET

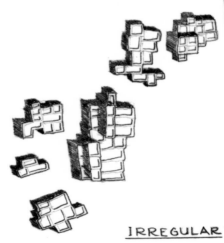

IRREGULAR

kiva, shrine, or religious marker was located there, the houses enclosing it and protecting it.

Plazas had a well-defined purpose in Pueblo lives but the nature of the site, the growth of the community, and other considerations often shaped the plan of the village. There might be more than one plaza. Plazas could be large and almost square, or they could be long and narrow. In some pueblos the buildings enclosed a central plaza or plazas. Other villages had rows of parallel house blocks in a streetlike arrangement, but the spaces between house rows were the plazas. Some villages had very irregular plans with one or more plazas and house blocks that did not seem to be aligned in any particular way.

How a Village Grew

When a settlement was originally built, the location of the kiva was probably decided and the first houses constructed around it. If the village was built on a level site and the surface of the land did not control where an excavation could be made, the kiva was given a predominant location. House clusters would form around the kiva site. On rocky mesa tops, kiva sites were determined by natural depressions in the surface, and the first groups of houses would cluster near this point if possible. Usually houses of people of the same clan were

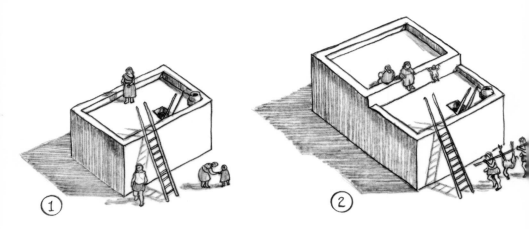

grouped together. To the original core, houses were added on, one by one, at different times. A few ancient ruins have been found that are so orderly and so symmetrical that there must have been a clearly fixed plan for their arrangement. For most pueblos, growth was gradual and lacked any definite plan.

As the daughters of the house married and more space was needed, an adjoining house was built on the side, or another house might be added in front of the first and a second story added to the original house. As rooms were surrounded and cut off from air and light, they became storerooms. When there was no more room for growth, a new house cluster would begin nearby. As new clans joined the pueblo, they were assigned locations for new house clusters. Each builder followed his or her own sense of the proper height and size for the room. The structure gradually took on a more uneven outline as buildings of slightly varying height were added at various places. If there were only sons in the family, no new houses would be built; even-

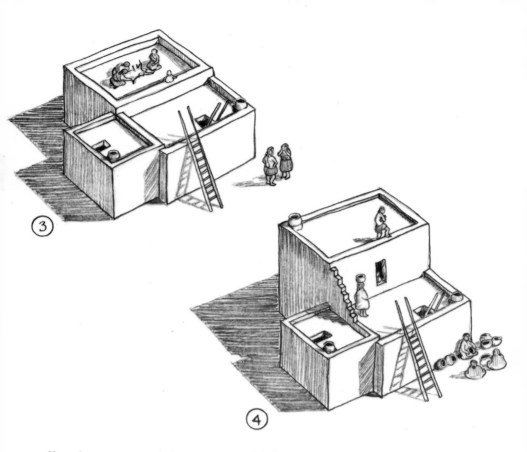

tually the parents' house would be empty. Over the years the clusters changed. Abandoned houses might be found in the midst of growing clusters.

Where houses were built in rows, the houses and their openings were arranged to secure sunny exposures and protection from wind and cold. Since much of the people's activities took place out on the terrace, terraces and doorways faced east or southeast to take advantage of the morning sunlight during winter months and to avoid the prevailing southwest winds.

5

6

A new village might be formed when the old one became too crowded. The Pueblo village system worked best with a fairly small population. The water supply and available farmland varied from village to village, but most pueblos could not support more than five hundred people. Sometimes a group might leave the pueblo after a dispute and start a new settlement. Or a summer farming village might grow and expand into a village apart from the main pueblo.

Community Life

The Pueblos lived an organized life with responsibilities and positions established by the community. Houses were all very much alike and about the same size. Everyone had about the same amount of food, clothing, and other material goods. There was not much privacy and not much desire for it. Nobody was supposed to stand out. Pueblos survived and prospered in a difficult environment by everyone working together, not by the achievements of individuals.

Pueblos were very busy places. On most days of the year old and young alike had their jobs to do, their contributions to make. No day was set aside as a day of rest, but everyday work stopped for festivals, rabbit hunts, corn husking, games, and other social events. Pueblo games were for everyone. They were an important part of life. Some were for fun, some were ceremonial. At certain seasons games were used to bring the rain, keep the sun moving, and even foretell the future.

The Pueblos traded with one another and with other Indian groups for thousands of years. Sometimes they went on trading expeditions, and sometimes others came to them, seeking their food and crafts. Trade also served as a means of getting news of other pueblos and other people.

Above all, pueblos were religious settlements. Care of the crops, hunting, war, public health, work, and play were accompanied by ceremonies that were just as important as the work or activity itself. Everything the Pueblo people did was part of their spiritual life and under the protection of the gods.

How the Pueblo Met the Needs of the Community

Pueblo people banded together for their mutual benefit. They developed a cycle of ceremonies and rituals that they believed were important to bring the rain, grow the corn, move the sun. The community was a necessary part of the religious system and the many ceremonies.

Corn was the foundation of Pueblo life. Without it the Pueblo way of life could not have survived. It may have accounted for as much as eighty percent of the Pueblos' diet. Corn was regarded with deep respect and reverence. Hardly a ceremony existed that did not use corn or corn meal in some way.

Corn cannot grow without water. Rain dances, as well as many other practices and prayers to bring the life-giving rain, were a regular part of life in the pueblo.

It is difficult to know the right time to plant crops, and in an area with such a short growing season, there was not much room for error. Each pueblo had an official Sun-Watcher who kept track of the movements of the sun for the community so people would know when to plant their corn and beans and when to harvest them. They also needed to know the approach of significant times in the cycle of sun movements, such as the winter solstice, and to know when it was time for dances and ceremonies. Announcements were made from the roof-tops to inform the people when important days were coming.

The spirit of unity and cooperation in pueblo communities made it possible for all to share whatever meager resources they had. The Pueblos were able to harmonize their material and spiritual culture and survived because each individual worked for the benefit of the community.

Pueblos Today

CHAPTER SIX

Descendants of the ancient Pueblos are still living in about thirty villages. Acoma and Old Oraibi are probably the only villages that are on the same sites they occupied when the Spanish first saw them. Most have been in the same general area, leaving a trail of ruins as the inhabitants changed location to find better defensive positions from the Spanish, or the Navaho, or to find more favorable farming conditions.

At the end of the nineteenth century the Pueblos were only beginning to be influenced by American culture. Their houses were still built in the style of their ancestors. A Pueblo family would have been able to move into a structure built hundreds of years earlier and make themselves at home.

As American contact increased through schools, missionaries, the Bureau of Indian Affairs, traders, anthropologists, and visitors, widespread changes began to take place in Pueblo settlements. Most Pueblos were faced with a conflict between adapting to new ways and preserving their own culture and the traditions that were important.

The population of the pueblos has been steadily increasing. As new housing was built, it no longer kept to traditional practices. Hatchways as the only means of entrance to a house no longer existed. Doors on the ground floor became the universal practice, but doors still were nearly always placed on the east or southeast side of the house. Windows were much larger and were usually made of glass. Villages expanded or new villages were constructed. Although a single room was still considered a complete house, separate single-family dwellings began to appear. Flat roofs became less common, and roofs on new buildings usually came to a peak or were shaped like a pyramid. New materials began to be used. The wood for roofs was almost all commercially bought lumber that had been pre-cut to standard sizes; tar paper and corrugated metal were frequently used as roofing materials.

Since World War II, cinderblocks have become the main building material. A single room is no longer considered a complete house; most houses have two or more rooms. Older houses have been remodeled to include a bathroom, kitchen, and other modern conveniences. Most of the upper stories have been abandoned. Pueblos today rarely have more than two stories. The covered passages that used to connect the plazas are open now. Pueblos are now reached by roads. Most have electricity, running water, and bottled gas. Tractors and threshers are seen in place of the ancient digging stick and carrying basket.

The Pueblos no longer need to build large, tightly clustered houses and villages on inaccessible sites for defense. New houses are built closer to crops, water, and flocks. The people have returned to a form of settlement that was common before the defensive village evolved — smaller groups living in scattered, small houses near springs and near the fields they cultivate. Many people live in houses on the outskirts of the village but also maintain a home in the old village. They regard the old village as a kind of spiritual headquarters and return there for special council meetings and ceremonies.

The Pueblos' spiritual life was based on a yearly cycle tied to an agricultural, corn-growing life. Now the need for money in the modern world forces the Pueblos to take outside jobs. The conflicts between the old way of life and the new way are still going on, but the Pueblo culture has stayed intact to a degree unique among Native Americans. Their way of life is changing, but they have managed to keep their vision focused on what has most value to them. As the villages become more modern, traditional things seem more important. People cling to the ceremonies and the ancient things hallowed by use. Every male dancer wears a handwoven kilt if he can get one; a Hopi bridegroom still receives his gift of corn meal on a handmade basket tray.

For some Pueblo people the old villages may be museums to look at from their suburban homes, but for most, community interaction is still very important. The old way of life goes on. They may change unimportant things like the clothing they wear and the kinds of houses they live in, but they continue to live their lives as part of the spiritual community of the pueblo.

Other Books About the Pueblo People

Erdoes, Richard. *The Rain Dance People: The Pueblo Indians, Their Past and Present.* New York: Knopf, 1976.
La Farge, Oliver. *A Pictorial History of the American Indian.* New York: Crown, 1956.
Tamarin, Alfred, and Shirley Glubok. *Ancient Indians of the Southwest.* Garden City: Doubleday, 1975.
Weiss, Malcolm E. *Sky Watchers of Ages Past.* Boston: Houghton Mifflin, 1982.

Bibliography

Adams, E. Charles. "The Architectural Analogue to Hopi Social Organization and Room Use, and Implications for Prehistoric Northern Southwestern Culture." *American Antiquity*, Vol. 48, No. 1 (January 1983), pp. 44–61.

Ambler, J. Richard. *The Anasazi*. Flagstaff: Museum of Northern Arizona Press, 1977.

Anderson, Edgar. "Maize of the Southwest." *Landscape*, Vol. 3, No. 2 (Winter 1953–54), pp. 26–27.

Arnold, David L. "Pueblo Pottery." *National Geographic*, Vol. 162, No. 5 (November 1982), pp. 593–605.

Beaglehole, Ernest. *Notes on Hopi Economic Life*. New Haven: Yale University Press, 1937 (Yale University Publications in Anthropology, No. 15). (Reprint, New York: AMS Press, 1978.)

Bradfield, Maitland. *The Changing Pattern of Hopi Agriculture*. London: Royal Anthropology Institute of Great Britain and Ireland, 1971 (Occasional Paper No. 30).

———. "Rodents of the Hopi Region, in Relation to Hopi Farming." *Plateau*, Vol. 44, No. 2 (Fall 1971), pp. 75–77.

Bryan, Kirk. "Flood-Water Farming." *Geographical Review*, No. 19 (1929), pp. 444–456.

Bunzel, Ruth L. *The Pueblo Potter: A Study of Creative Imagination in Primitive Art*. New York: Columbia University Press, 1929. (Reprint, New York: Dover Publications, 1972.)

———, ed. "Zuñi Texts." *American Ethnological Society*, Vol. 15 (1933), pp. 1–13.

Canby, Thomas Y. "The Anasazi: Riddles in the Ruins." *National Geographic*, Vol. 162, No. 5 (November 1982), pp. 554–592.

Curtis, William E. *Children of the Sun*. Chicago: Inter-Ocean Publishing Co., 1883. (Reprint, New York: AMS Press, 1976.)

Fewkes, J. Walter. "The Sun's Influence on the Form of Hopi Pueblos." *American Anthropologist*, n.s., Vol. 8 (1906), pp. 88–100.

Fitch, James Marston, and Daniel P. Branch. "Primitive Architecture and Climate." *Scientific American,* Vol. 203, No. 6 (December 1960), pp. 134–144.

Forde, C. Daryll. *Habitat, Economy and Society.* New York: Dutton, 1934, pp. 220–259.

Frost, Richard H. "The Romantic Inflation of Pueblo Culture." *American West,* Vol. 17, No. 1 (1980), pp. 5–9, 56–60.

Guthe, Carl E. *Pueblo Pottery Making: A Study at the Village of San Ildefonso.* New Haven: Yale University Press, 1925. (Reprint, New York: AMS Press, 1980.)

Harrison, S. G., G. B. Masefield, and Michael Wallis. *The Oxford Book of Food Plants.* London: Oxford University Press, 1969.

Hawley, Florence. "The Family Tree of Chaco Canyon Masonry." *American Antiquity,* Vol. 3 (1937–38), pp. 247–255.

Hewett, Edgar L. *Ancient Life in the American Southwest.* Indianapolis: Bobbs-Merrill, 1930.

———— and Bertha P. Dutton. *The Pueblo Indian World.* Albuquerque: University of New Mexico Press, 1945 (Handbooks of Archaeological History).

Horgan, Paul. "Place, Form and Prayer: The Prehistoric Human Geography of the Town Indians of the Rio Grande." *Landscape,* Vol. 3, No. 2 (Winter 1953–54), pp. 7–11.

Jackson, John B. "Essential Architecture." *Landscape,* Vol. 10, No. 3 (Spring 1961), pp. 27–30.

————. "Pueblo Architecture and Our Own." *Landscape,* Vol. 3, No. 2 (Winter 1953–54), pp. 20–25.

Lambert, Marjorie F. "Cities Before Columbus: Prehistoric Town Planning in the Puebloan Southwest." *Landscape,* Vol. 3, No. 2 (Winter 1953–54), pp. 12–15.

Laxalt, Robert. "New Mexico: The Golden Land." *National Geographic,* Vol. 138, No. 3 (September 1970), pp. 299–345.

McCluskey, Stephen C. "The Astronomy of the Hopi Indians." *Journal for the History of Astronomy,* Vol. 8, Part 3, No. 23 (October 1977), pp. 174–195.

McGregor, John C. *Southwestern Archaeology,* 2d ed. Urbana: University of Illinois Press, 1965.

McIntire, Elliot G. "Changing Patterns of Hopi Indian Settlement." *Annals of the Association of American Geographers,* Vol. 61, No. 3 (1971), pp. 510–521.

Mangelsdorf, Paul C. *Corn: Its Origin, Evolution, and Improvement.* Cambridge: Belknap Press of Harvard University Press, 1974.

Mauzy, Wayne. "Architecture of the Pueblos." *El Palacio,* Vol. 42, Nos. 4, 5, 6 (1937), pp. 21–30.

Mindeleff, Victor. *A Study of Pueblo Architecture in Tusayan and Cibola.* Washington, D.C.: Smithsonian Institution, 1891 (Eighth Annual Report of the Bureau of American Ethnology).

Mora, Joseph Jacinto. *The Year of the Hopi.* Washington, D.C.: Smithsonian Institution, 1979.

Page, Susanne, and Jake Page. *Hopi*. New York: Harry N. Abrams, 1982.

———. "Inside the Sacred Hopi Homeland." *National Geographic*, Vol. 162, No. 5 (November 1982), pp. 607–629.

Qoyawayma, Polingaysi. *No Turning Back*. Albuquerque: University of New Mexico Press, 1964.

Rapoport, Amos. *House, Form, and Culture*. Englewood Cliffs: Prentice-Hall, 1969.

Roediger, Virginia More. *Ceremonial Costumes of the Pueblo Indians*. Berkeley: University of California Press, 1941.

Schroeder, Albert H. "Man and Environment in the Verde Valley." *Landscape*, Vol. 3, No. 2 (Winter 1953–54), pp. 16–19.

Scully, Vincent. *Pueblo: Mountain, Village, Dance*. New York: Viking, 1975.

Sedgwick, Mrs. William T. *Acoma, the Sky City*. Cambridge: Harvard University Press, 1926.

Shapiro, Harry L. *Homes Around the World*. New York: American Museum of Natural History, 1945.

Simmons, Leo W., ed. *Sun Chief: The Autobiography of a Hopi Indian*. New Haven: Yale University Press, 1942.

Stanislawski, Michael B. "What Good Is a Broken Pot? An Experiment in Hopi-Tewa Ethno-Archaeology." *Southwestern Lore*, Vol. 35, No. 1 (June 1969), pp. 11–18.

Stewart, Guy R. "Conservation in Pueblo Agriculture: I. Primitive Practices." *Scientific Monthly*, Vol. 51 (September 1940), pp. 201–220.

———. "Conservation in Pueblo Architecture: II. Present-Day Flood Water Irrigation." *Scientific Monthly*, Vol. 51 (October 1940), pp. 329–340.

Stubbs, Stanley A. *Bird's-Eye View of the Pueblos*. Norman: University of Oklahoma Press, 1950.

Sturtevant, William C., general ed., and Alfonso Ortiz, volume ed. *Southwest*. Washington, D.C., Smithsonian Institution, 1979 (Handbook of North American Indians, Vol. 9).

Underhill, Ruth. *Pueblo Crafts*. Washington, D.C.: U.S. Indian Service, 1945 (American Handicrafts, No. 7). (Reprint, New York: AMS Press, 1979.)

———. *Work A Day Life of the Puebloes*. Washington, D.C.: U.S. Indian Service, 1946 (Indian Life and Customs, No. 4).

Wenger, Gilbert R. *The Story of Mesa Verde National Park*. Mesa Verde National Park: Mesa Verde Museum Association, 1980.

White, Jon Manchip. *Everyday Life of the North American Indian*. New York: Holmes & Meier, 1979.

Whorf, Benjamin Lee. *Language, Thought, and Reality*. Cambridge: MIT Press, 1956.

Willey, Gordon R., ed. *Prehistoric Settlement Patterns in the New World*. New York: Viking Fund, 1956 (Viking Fund Publications in Anthropology, Vol. 23).

Winkler, William C. *Mesa Verde*. Cortez: Interpark, 1977.

Index